I Grew Where
I Was Planted

CORNELIA ELMORE

ISBN 978-1-63961-287-1 (paperback)
ISBN 978-1-63961-288-8 (digital)

Christian Faith Publishing
832 Park Avenue
Meadville, PA 16335
www.christianfaithpublishing.com

Printed in the United States of America

Devoted to anyone who has ever perceived or believed that God has His hand on your life and that the rest of your life isn't your own to do with it as you choose—that the journey will be lonely, many times misunderstood by many, and yet extremely rewarding (Luke 9:23–24).

If you are reading this book, then you have this charge upon your life! Be of good courage.

"Trust in the Lord with all your heart; and lean not unto your own understanding. In all of your ways acknowledge Him and He shall direct your paths" (Proverbs 3:5–6).

Contents

I Grew Where I Was Planted

Blessed is the man that walketh not in the counsel of the ungodly, nor standeth in the way of sinners, nor sitteth in the seat of the scornful. But his delight is in the law of the *Lord*; and in his law doth he meditate day and night. And he *shall be like a tree planted by the rivers of water,* that bringeth forth his fruit in his season; his leaf also shall not wither; and whatsoever he doeth shall prosper. (Psalm 1:1–3)

CORNELIA ELMORE

When I Was a Child

I began to think about love and life at an early age, how much fun it would be to grow up like my parents, in true love and devotion toward each other. They did not argue; if they did, not in front of the children. They were always together: going to the grocery store, church services, or shopping for the kids. Dad would go to work every day early, and Mother would make his lunch as he would eat his daily prepared hot breakfast, drinking Sanka decaf coffee together and talking about what her day would consist of with the children. Mother was a stay-at-home mom and loved every moment. He would always kiss her before he would leave. Mother never learned how to drive, but Dad was a dedicated husband/father. My uncle, mother's baby brother, got into a fatal car crash, and Mother took it very hard. Though she was not afraid of driving, she just didn't put any further effort into it after my uncle's accident.

The holidays were the best! Thanksgiving, Easter, Christmas, and our birthdays were celebrated in style. We enjoyed eating! Mother was a semi-professional chef and did not even know it. She could prepare meals that not only melted in your mouth but would wake up the senses of the people from around the neighborhood with such delicious aroma. Turkey and corn bread dressing with gravy, beef pot roast with potatoes, carrots, celery, and onions. When there were familiar people who passed away, she would always bake a cake or a dish of food for the family to help ease the stress of out-of-town guests. Dad would hand-churn his extremely excellent homemade vanilla ice cream, which was the best! He used this old seafoam green ice cream bucket and would churn and add blocks of hard ice and salt around the base of it—soooo very good. Dad grew up in the south and was a hunter since a child. He and his brother-in-law would go to "the woods" and hunt rabbit, squirrel, raccoon, pheasant, and quail—a hunter he was! Not only would he hunt but also fish; he loved to fish and was extremely good at both.

We went to church every Sunday as a family, regardless of what the previous night had planned for growing teenage girls. Our parents were good-standing members in the church (deacon and deaconess), which held a degree of responsibility and pride. You did not act out of character, and if by some *out-of-body experience that you did*, well, there were consequences that you would pay. Time-outs were not the normal course of consequences. They had a rule: "spare the rod and spoil the child"—we were *not* spoiled, let's just say.

I was the middle child of three, and my sister was older and a gentle soul. Matter of fact, she was a preemie. We got along well. We had no other choice; our parents were not having it any other way. Remember, there would be consequences! Our beloved brother came years later. So the three of us grew up in a loving and caring household with parents who kept a roof over our head, food on the table, clothes on our backs, and a couple of nickels that we could have a family outing at the local Burger Chef for an occasional cheeseburger treat. I thought it was the best of the best of life—if we were poor, I did not know it.

As I started into my teenage years, around sixteen to eighteen, I felt that those were stressful times for me. I had an extreme case of facial blemishes, blackheads, and pimples. Nothing helped! We tried creams, ointments, even old family myths—baby diaper urine and lemons wrapped in a clean white cloth, heated then applied to the face. It made me feel self-conscious and embarrassed to speak up when I had the correct answer to questions in the classroom. I found myself inwardly feeling isolated. Of course, I was not, but this was when the enemy of my soul (Satan) started speaking to me. High school was an educational experience and a lot of fun. I was an average student and well-liked by many.

When I was about six years old, I was playing around a lamp that didn't have a covering or a shade over it, and the bulb was exposed.

Mother said, "Don't play too close to the lamp. I don't need it to fall on you."

Those words no sooner came out of her mouth, and the lamp fell on my forehead. The bulb was so hot that it literally took the flesh from my forehead, and Mother was beside me, crying, "Oh my baby, oh my baby—" then the supernatural happened. The forehead flesh came back as if it was never removed by the bulb. Mother gasped for her breath and said, "My God, my God, look at that!" I just sat there, no pain, no emotion, no words—just looked at her and smiled, not really knowing what just happened.

Dad came home from work, and they went into the bedroom to discuss things. She had the light bulb in her hands (where the flesh had become hard on it). I could hear her saying something about "her forehead." Then Dad came out of the room, grabbed me by the arm, and looked at my forehead intensely.

He said, "I don't see anything."

Mother said, "And you won't. God did a miracle."

He asked me how I felt, and I said, "Okay."

As believers in Christ, we understood God could do all things! This, however, was something special. It was then and as I grew older that I would experience "the hand of God over my life."

"The thief (Satan) comes not, but to steal, and to kill, and to destroy" (John 10:10).

God had other plans; praise His Holy Name!

As I grew older, around eighteen to twenty-one, I wanted to experience "life" on my own terms, so I searched for an apartment. Growing up in a religious family atmosphere, there were restrictions. Our parents were from the "ole school." "We don't want you staying out past 1:00 a.m., get married, and then have children. Don't use drugs/alcohol, and by all means, don't live with a man whom you are not married to." Of course, there's not one thing wrong with these moral values. I was the experimental type. Don't misunderstand me, I could see another person doing something and not have to go down that path. However, there were other fun things. Well, I just wanted to see how it was for myself.

One day, out of nowhere, this voice said to me, "You will never have a man love you like your father loved your mother." Of course, I knew who that was, the enemy of my soul. I had just recently broken up with a very favorite person, and it was difficult.

"No man will love you. They will only use you," that ugly voice spoke.

Unfortunately, I had just thought that love would flee from me like leprosy. Not trying to hear that voice of the enemy, I played another video scene in my mind, one that there *would* be a love for me.

Days, weeks, months passed by, and that sickening feeling of loneliness had set in, taking up residence, renting space in my head, and having a pity party. I decided that I was going to have some fun. I found myself getting dressed and going out! Going out on the town by myself. I went to a couple of spots where I knew people and they knew me, you know that spot where everyone knows your name. Met with a few new friends and talked about life. Had a few good laughs, drinks, and dances—went home, alone.

The ugly voice met me at the door of my apartment. "Still alone, huh?"

Completely ignored it and went to sleep.

Sunday church services were dry and boring. The songs we sang, I didn't understand why we would even sing such sad songs. If Jesus Christ has done so many marvelous things for us and died while doing it, then why are we singing like we're crying? But I went because I felt better about myself, and I saw my family/friends there. Remember, I grew up in a religious household—a Christian atmosphere having the knowledge of God but not a relationship with God.

It was difficult to have a relationship with God when you thought He was judging you all the time. We feared and revered God for who He is, not knowing Him for all that He has done through Jesus Christ. I wouldn't experience a relationship with God until many years later, when I became a believer in Jesus Christ. Growing up as a child in my parents' household, we believed as they did. The foundation of a Christian life is what parents are to supply to their children. It is the fervent responsibility to "seek the Lord while He can be found" for any person to individually grow in Christ.

"Today, if you will hear His voice, harden not your heart" (Psalm 95:8).

When I Became an Adult

"When I was a child, I spoke as a child, I understood as a child, I thought as a child: but when I became a man, I put away childish things" (1 Corinthians 13:11).

Believing the supernatural realm was not unusual for me. I touted myself as a believer, but to commit to saying a Christian, well, that was not what I was willing to admit to—yet!

While working at a prosperous worldwide corporation, I became friends with many influential people. I got exposed to areas of life that most people only view in a magazine; my outgoing personality was contagious! After a while, I became intimately involved with a man who was "too good to be true." We had a long and exciting relationship, and then we ended it—mutually. There arose such an intense conviction from my heart that I had never experienced before! The conviction was that of a cheating wife on her husband; mind you, I'm not married, but very single. It was persistent, almost nagging. I did not know where it was coming from other than within my soul. Knowing that prayer changes things, I began to pray and seek, really seek, God. I spoke to my mother, who knew how to get a prayer through to God. She told me that she would pray for me as well. The power of a praying mother!

One morning, after entertaining overnight company, I had a supernatural experience that brought me to my knees, literally. I was setting on the side of my bed, sobbing and saying to my heart, "Is this all there is to life? A one-night stand, no real love—nothing to hold onto?" I was in a bad state of being—of my own making.

Then, immediately, the literal sun from the sky came into my bedroom, and the voice said, "Get saved!"

The brightness of His presence was above the sun's rays— beyond brilliant bright. He said it again, "Get saved!"

I didn't know what *saved* meant, but it would be my mission to find out. I fell to my knees, dried up my tears, and praised the Lord with my whole heart, soul, and mind! I thanked God for visiting me and telling me what to do! I thanked God for His relentless love and care over me and anything else that came to my mind—I was set free!

It was the beginning of a new week. I went to work, and while walking across the corporation parking lot, one of my friends yelled and said, "Are you saved?" I said *no*, but whatever saved is, I need to be it!

As she approached me closer, she gave me a big hug and explained how that last evening, while at church in prayer, she saw me in a vision (she was a real, saved, tongue-talking Holy

Ghost-filled Christian) and that the Lord told her to seek me out tomorrow. She invited me to her church service on Wednesday, September 25, 1985, at 8:31 p.m.

I got saved! Glory to God, I got saved and filled with the Holy Ghost with the evidence of speaking in other tongues as the Spirit of the Lord gives the utterance. My spiritual birthday and my natural birthday are the two dates you don't forget.

Well, the persistent nagging conviction went away, and now I understand what is was: "*My sheep hear my voice and they know me and they follow me*" (John 10:27).

God was calling me to salvation through Jesus Christ, and the conviction was His calling card to get my attention. God pulled on my heartstrings. I'm so glad He loved me to keep me from going over into the abyss.

"*For I know the thoughts that I think toward you, saith the Lord. Thoughts of peace and not of evil. To give you an expected end*" (Jeremiah 29:11).

I did not entertain any more overnight guests, because the love that I had in my heart for Jesus Christ wouldn't allow me to betray my *love!*

My spiritual mother put time into helping me develop the foundation that a warrior would need. She had discerned God's hand upon my life to the extent that battle in many arenas would be normal; she also was a warrior. We would have Bible studies—group session Bible study, church weekday Bible study—wherever they were holding a serious Bible study, we went. We had to feed the spirit and starve the flesh in order to grow in the things of God.

Hearing God's Voice

Have you ever heard the voice of God speak to you? Of course you have, and not recognized it. Remember when you would go against "that first thought"? The gut was telling you that this is the right way—go this way! *But* you did not. That was the voice of God leading you into the proper path to take. How do I know that to be fact? Glad you asked. God will *never* take second place to you in anything that you do; He *is God*, the creator of all things—our Creator. "So God created man in his *own* image, in the image of God created he him; male and female created he them" (Genesis 1:27).

Of course, He (God) has *all* wisdom to connect to His children. Almighty God can get to us in ways that we can't comprehend. He is supernatural, and we are not! There, literally, isn't anywhere in the universe that He can't reach us—ask Jonah. Jonah 1:3 reads:

> But Jonah rose up to flee unto Tarshish
> from the presence of the LORD, and went
> down to Joppa; and he found a ship going to

Tarshish: so he paid the fare thereof, and went down into it, to go with them unto Tarshish from the presence of the LORD.

Note how Jonah tried to flee from the presence of God by running in the opposite direction. The place where Jonah found himself was in the belly of the beast. We oftentimes find ourselves fleeing a situation that is not what our initial intentions are, just to turn around and start over. Finding ourselves in the belly of the beast could mean lost to an addiction, a tumultuous damaging relationship, out of the will of God, strife and unforgiveness—a myriad of other issues that take the U-turn from the ultimate direction God has for our destiny.

While experiencing literally the time of my life at the late Dr. Kenneth E. Hagin's meeting in Tulsa, Oklahoma, in 1987, the presence of the Lord fell like rain fire from heaven! We were dancing around the room, praising the Lord, speaking in tongues. What an experience in the Lord. Dr. Hagin had a prophecy about the end of time and the church. I'd never experienced such a move of God, what a time! I knew that I was in the presence of His Majesty!

I heard, from inside myself, from the belly upwards "*I AM the Lord, and I change NOT!*"

The voice of God spoke to me so strong that I sat down in my chair to hear whatever would come next. Then God said, "*I have chosen you for such a time as this, fear not, for I am always with you.*"

Be still!

I found myself, for months, being still. Being still from engaging in trying to, in my own self, make stuff happen! You know how it is when we want to go ahead and move in our own minds, trying to get ahead of the game. Thinking that if I move this money or accept this position without praying about, maybe it would develop and turn out right for me. Just to find out that it (whatever it is) wasn't what it looked like. Being deceived by your own thoughts. God's ways are hard to figure out, that's why we always need to pray and ask for our next steps to be ordered by the Lord. God will order your footsteps in the way that they should go! The Word of God says that the footsteps of a righteous man are ordered by the Lord.

My desert experience

It was 2003. I had a short and brief three-year marriage to a person that I hand-picked. God didn't pick him for me. Loneliness and lack of companionship had set in. The truth be told, he had a serious drug abuse problem, to say the least. This arrogant and self-centered selection of a lifelong spouse turned into an expensive and painful heartbreaking form of marital existence. This person was classified as a "functional addict," according to many doctors. You would never, in a million years, believe he could do the things he did, never! The old saying "looks are deceiving" is a total understatement for this individual.

For a special congratulatory gift of ministry, my family gave me a monetary gift to assist the purchase of a car that I had my eye on for a while. After purchasing the vehicle, my husband wrecked it while on a three-day drug binge, only before abandoning the rental car, in an empty parking lot, that had been riddled with bullets on the driver's side.

This seemed so overwhelming to look at someone whom your heart just goes out to, in love for this person, and there is not a thing you can do to stop them from their destructive path. So after many AA meetings, sober/clean sessions, and therapists, he was still the same ole, same ole—he had not hit rock bottom yet.

While researching the internet on another unrelated topic, I came across a six-month $100,000 substance abuse clinical trial that was being hosted at the Stanford University Hospital and Clinics in Stanford, California. This got my attention, and I further read how to meet the eligibility criteria.

First, the candidate had to have a proven history of substance abuse (documented by professionals); second, the candidate had to be over twenty-one years old; and finally, the candidate had to have a relative(s) who lived in California for over three years whom the candidate could stay/live with until the trial was completed. There would be a monthly stipend of $500 awarded to the relative(s) for allowing the candidate to stay in the home.

Yes, he met the eligibility criteria on each item. Now it would be a challenge to convince him that this would be required in order to continue in our marriage. We had a very intense conversation and came to the better judgment it was necessary. We had an "awkward" love for one another, but loved each other nevertheless. Our vows meant the world to me; for him, well, not so much. Don't marry someone who really doesn't believe in God the way you do; you'll find yourself *unequally yoked* (2 Corinthians 6:14).

We called his family in California and discussed the situation with them. After several days had gone past, they called us back and gave us the news that "they will allow this process on certain terms." His family has had this battle with him for over five years, at least. This, however, was the first time his wife got involved to this extent. I was his third marriage—that I did not know until this point in our relationship, and it was shocking.

The family stated that there will be *no* using in their home, period. If this should occur, we will be immediately kicked out! We then began to plot out our timetable to meet them in California. Two weeks and three days later, we were on the road to California.

The desert seemed so dry, alone, and desolate. You may ask, "What desert?" Glad you asked. California. The desert is where God will drive you to in order to go through it and be tried by issues that only a distant land can afford. Also, out of the heart is where issues will crop up and ask, "What about me?" I knew *not one person*—not one! No one whom I could go to just to get away from in-laws. Remember Father Abraham (Genesis 12:1). Even while meeting the in-laws, no familiar connection. Nice enough people, just no connection.

After getting settled into the home, it wasn't two months past that he didn't find a way to use. The family did not know about it, but I did. While dropping me off to work, he'd go find "the boys" who used. Dope friends are everywhere, and if you are one, you'll find their cove. He drove over forty minutes one way to get to them, being late practically every day in picking me up from work. I stand waiting, so utterly embarrassed by passing by coworkers who had gotten off over forty-five minutes, the same time I did.

It took about four months total to be finally kicked out of the house. The stipend did come in handy for the family.

We had *no place* to go but to the VA homeless shelter of California.

Homeless shelter living

Have you ever had "a thing" that you dreaded would happen to you? Being bitten/eaten by a shark while swimming in the ocean, riding a roller coaster and falling from it, drowning, hang gliding and the parachute comes apart, flying in an airplane and it crashes—homelessness was my "thing."

My personal prayer was "Please, God, don't ever allow me to be homeless." (Be aware that which you fear may come upon you.) I believe that every woman, especially women, have prayed that prayer. To live in your own space and place has been my life's motto, "Pay where you lay." Wherever you lay your head should be secure, safe, and comfortable.

That became my reality, a Veteran's homeless shelter for the next six to eight months of my life. He did not use in this facility but stayed clean, for at least six months. There were counselors and clinicians along with meeting after meeting after meeting that he had to report to.

Then I divorced him! I had *enough*! That was one of the most emotional and upsetting days of my entire life. I served him papers, in front of the entire unit, and he got on a bus and left. That was the last time that I saw him. I felt like an anvil was lifted from my chest; I could breathe again, really breathe free from that choking, fearful hold that crushed my heart. In my own way, unto God in the secret place of my heart, I vowed that I would not ever seek another man again, if God didn't place him in my path.

My prayers for him (my ex) have always been that before he departs this life, eternally, that he become a Christian—a lover of Jesus Christ—the way Christ loves him. If only he could grasp that kind of agape love that comes from a loving Father. That love would change any person. It did for me. But no one comes unto God unless He draws you to Himself.

Not too long after leaving that shelter did I join alone another shelter that allowed women/children to get on their feet. *This was godsent.* That was where I was told by the Holy Spirit, "*Grow where you are planted.*" I did not understand the meaning, but for sure, God was going to show me *exactly* what He meant.

I made friends with a man, a former Marine and a down-right "*good man*" who befriended me in ways that only God will ever know! I believe this person, not perfect (no one is), was directed by God into my life as a California guardian. It sounds crazy, but California is another plant that has people of another world! Their ways of life are so very different from the Midwest where I grew up. I now believe he was sent for safety, companionship, and maneuvering through the state of California. To this day we remain *true friends.*

Think deep before you leap!

Here's the thing: when seeking a life partner, there are characteristics that govern a person's thinking. What is his/her stance in Christ: strong, weak, mediocre? Do they even have a particular stance? How can I develop a meaningful Christian relationship with this person and not be carnal? Carnality, in its proper place, can work as normal; human progression, but out of place, can lead to disastrous and insulting actions.

Praying always, in every situation, should be the normal. When God has been given an invitation to conduct your affairs, they always are the best.

After being divorced/single for many years, God has placed a person in my path, from my church—a beautiful divorced/single man of God that I am able to pray with, talk to about any and everything, trust and believe to see prayers answered, *no* judgement zone. *Praise the Lord!* And of course, go out to dinner and a movie!

"Many are the afflictions of the righteous, but the Lord delivers us out of them all" (Psalm 34:19).

This passage of scripture has been one of my most trusted and leaned upon ones. This particular scripture has settled my concerns, frets, and even worries. Yes, worries. *"Casting all your care upon him; for he careth for you"* (1 Peter 5:7) became very real to me.

When I served my ex with divorce papers, it was a depressing day. Never in a lifetime did I think that divorce would be in my destiny. But when we take matters of the hearts into our own hands and think that we know better than God, well, guess what? You get what you get—trouble and heartaches.

"He heals the brokenhearted and binds up all their wounds" (Psalm 147:3).

God did not lead or place my former husband in my path; I did that, all by myself. I should have known better than to try to find a husband, when the Word of God is clear: *"he that finds a wife...*" So the marriage lasted three years, long enough for me to experience the *trip* of a lifetime.

The marriage was so deceptive that the enemy of my soul found me a *joke*. But God had a better plan. God turned all of my sorrows, all of my tears into a learning experience and bottled all of my tears. God gave me treasures in my pain, treasures of darkness.

I Will Guide You

I began my journey in a land where I literally knew *no one*. (Former in-laws had dismissed me and wanted nothing to do with me.) Remember, I relocated from Ohio to California while being married. I felt like Abraham, when God told him, "I will lead you from your *father's house* to a land...*that you know not of*."

Note: Father's house refers to from the familiar to the desert land the absolute unfamiliar!

I was inwardly fearful but knew in my heart of hearts that failure, going back home, wasn't an option. Have you ever had that "come-to-Jesus moment" that you knew what is ahead of you will change you forever? That's what I knew was about to take place.

It became apparent to me that this was a learning and developing situation. The Word of the Lord, as I studied daily, came to me saying, "As you fervently seek me daily for guidance, direction, and life lessons, you will be guided by a soft leading of the Holy Spirit as to what and where you need to go. You'll never be alone, you'll never be unsafe, you'll never be misguided! I don't play games about your life. I've told you that in Jeremiah 29:11–13:

> For I know the thoughts that I think toward you, saith the LORD, thoughts of peace, and not of evil, to give you an expected end. Then shall ye call upon me, and ye shall go and pray unto me, and I will hearken unto you. And ye shall seek me, and find me, when ye shall search for me with all your heart.

Once you get the understanding that our Heavenly Father loves you unconditionally, cares for you affectionately, and is watchful over you daily and every point in life—as minute as the day to day grind may seem to you—watched over like a bird watches her baby birds taking their first flight, *then,* and only then, will you become emboldened to walk upright in strength and power. Not, of course, in *your* might, but in the might of His Majesty, *God.* As well as knowing that *God* is never mad at you, ever!

To know that *God,* the master of the universe; *God,* who made the whole earth, the oceans and the seas, and the fullness thereof, the cattle on a thousand hills; *God,* who is the creator of the sun, the moon, and the stars; *God,* who spread the expanse of the sky by spreading out His hand; *God, the I am that I am*—Moses's *God*—Glory to His name!

When this fact becomes the reality that you live from one day to the next, success on levels you have never met will be manifested in your life.

Don't be confused to think that this type of newly found and forged lifestyle will fall onto you like ripe cherries off a tree, without resistance from Satan; it will not! The enemy of your soul will torment, tease, temp, and terrify you at every opportunity.

It is in the *dry spaces*. Being unsatisfied with your partner/spouse, your income/job, your appearance, even your food intake—these are *dry spaces*.

It is in those dry spaces that the evil, sinister, and demonic enemy of our soul torments us the most. The unsatisfied this or the unsatisfied that. He'll talk to your mind about making sudden and sporadic decisions that will be regretted later.

Remember Luke 4:1–5, when the tempter, Satan, was speaking with our Lord in the desert, at Christ's most vulnerable point—hunger. When Jesus had been led in the desert by the Holy Ghost to be tried of the devil after, He had fasted forty days and forty nights. It is at that point, whatever your dry space—your unfulfilled desire is—that's when he, Satan, will pounce.

The Word of God says that "he acts like a roaring lion…"

The Conflict

Wherefore the law is holy, and the commandment holy, and just, and good. Was then that which is good made death unto me? God forbid. But sin, that it might appear sin, working death in me by that which is good; that sin by the commandment might become exceedingly sinful. For we know that the law is spiritual: but I am carnal, sold under sin. For that which I do I allow not: for what I would, that I do not; but what I hate, that do I. If then I do that which I would not, I consent unto the law that it is good. Now then it is no longer I that do it, but sin that dwelleth in me. For I know that in me (that is, in my flesh,) dwelleth no good thing: for to will is present with me; but how to perform that which is good I find not. (Romans 7:12–18)

As long as mankind exists, as long as we have morals, thoughts, and emotions, we will have a mental battle between good and evil. This fact doesn't make you evil; it's our nature. The change comes through the process of being "born again."

While many of us battle within ourselves to do good versus evil, it is a moment-to-moment, day-to-day process. Don't deceive yourself to think that your flesh is any different from anyone else's—it is *not*.

The same temptations that one person experiences are the same that *all* people experience. Jesus said in His word, "With the same temptation that you have experienced, I have as well, experienced." Jesus, being God in the flesh, with all power, supernatural, has gone through it!

With the aforementioned being stated, the day-to-day battle continues. The constant conflict is not only frustratingly tiresome but exhausting.

So now the question becomes, what can we do to *stop* the tormenting conflict? Glad you asked! We bring every thought captive before the Word of God. The Word of God is the X-ray that will evaluate what is promise or purpose. With various thoughts battling for territorial space in our minds, we need a sifter that can rightly divide (separate) the needed from dross.

Each thought that floats in the atmosphere isn't necessarily a thought that you should give credence to.

The Inglewood California Experience

In 1986 or so, my spiritual daughter and I were in Inglewood, California, walking the streets under an anointing from the Lord. We had no clue why or where we were headed, only that the Lord had His hand upon us in a mighty way. Little did we know that this day would change, literally, the spiritual outlook on our lives.

While we were walking and talking about our next steps, we suddenly saw Doctors Kenneth Hagin Sr., Frederick KC Price, and Kenneth Copeland (and their wives Betty, Betty, and Gloria) standing in a parking lot, fellowshipping.

We walked over to them to speak to them, and Dr. Hagin said, "Come to the meeting this afternoon, and sit in the front row." We said we will and went about our day.

Later on that evening, we were so excited about the instructions that we had been given; we got to the church about one hour ahead of time and sat in the front row, just like Dr. Hagin had instructed us.

It was a camp meeting environment. Over one thousand folks had to have been there—what a time!

We had not experienced such an outpouring of the presence of God *ever*!

What the enemy intended for bad, God turned it around for His good!

"For we know that all things work together for the good, to those who love the Lord and are called according to His purpose" (Romans 8:28).

"And I will give you treasures of darkness and hidden riches of secret places, that you may know that I, the God of Israel, have called you by your name" (Isaiah 45:3).

About the Author

While growing up in the Midwest, the middle of three children, Cornelia knew in her heart that each person was placed on earth by design—to grow and develop into what God Almighty had predestined us to. How she knew that, well, she took a look around! Everyone was so different. Her quest had been to define "what am I to accomplish for God while on this earth?" Hence, the purpose for this book, *I Grew Where I Was Planted*. She was planted in the family she grew up with to accomplish a divine cause.

In writing this book, she took deep inspection of what is the purpose of our upbringing: our parents, our education, even our relocating from state to state. The timing of it all. Is it of our own permitting, or is God orchestrating and guiding us for His glory? She felt as if she was like a tender green plant that grew through extremely hard soil (the world), attempting to reach the warmth of sunlight for survival and nourishment.

In the latter years of her life, at age sixty-five, she is seeking the purpose of this great plan of God. Whether or not she arrives at a destination is not the question. Instead, *when*, in her heart, has she accomplished her purpose is her reward.

She thanks everyone for taking this journey with her, for she couldn't do it alone.

CPSIA information can be obtained
at www.ICGtesting.com
Printed in the USA
LVHW010734220322
714055LV00002B/234